HOW GOOD AND HOW PLEASANT IT IS
The Importance and Power of Unity

Jamal E. Quinn

Table of Contents

DEDICATION

This book is dedicated first and foremost to my LORD and Savior Jesus Christ who has given me great grace to write this book, and to share his heart as it relates to unity in the Body of Christ.

It is also dedicated to all the men and woman in the Body of Christ who understand the importance of unity, and have unified in the faith to do the perfect will of God.

I am also thankful to the people of God who have unified and labored with me in the preaching and teaching of the Gospel of the Kingdom.

Last but not least, it is dedicated to my wife of over 33 years, Sheryl Lynn Quinn, in whom I found love and unity when we were only teenagers in high school. Thank you for standing by me through all the tests, trials, tribulations and triumphs which have made us strong! To all of the faithful Firm Foundation members, who labor and serve faithfully with me in the work of the ministry, thank you for your servitude and service in Jesus Name! May God bless you richly!

INTRODUCTION

Unity is one of the most important doctrines in the Bible. There are so many scriptures in the Bible that continuously exhort us to unify, but for some reason many in the Body of Christ have found it very difficult to unify as a Body of believers. Of course we know that this is not the entire body of Christ, but for the most part we have found it very difficult to maintain consistent unity according to scripture. Not only that, but there is a demonic spirit of pride and division that has engulfed the United States where we see different groups of people unifying for the purpose of dividing the nation.

I want you to know that it is God's will that the true Church and ecclesia who are the Body of Christ unify to be the light of the world. How can we as a church be the light of the world, the salt of the earth or a city on a hill that cannot be hidden, if we are divided?

If we desire to experience the unprecedented Pentecost power and anointing of God, and the abundant blessings that he desires to pour out upon his people, we would be wise to be not only hearers of the Word but doers! Where there is no unity, there is division. Where there is division there is no strength. Please go with me as we journey through the scriptures see what the Bible has to say concerning unity and oneness in the Bible and among the people of God

CHAPTER 1

A SYNOPSIS OF PSALM 133

Psalms 133:1-3 KJV
1 A Song of degrees of David. Behold, how good and how pleasant it is for brethren to dwell together in unity!
2 It is like the precious ointment upon the head, that ran down upon the beard, even Aaron's beard: that went down to the skirts of his garments;
3 As the dew of Hermon, and as the dew that descended upon the mountains of Zion: for there the LORD commanded the blessing, even life for evermore.

Psalm 133 is a wonderful Psalm written by our beloved King David who was a man after God's own heart. David wrote many psalms which where an expression of his love for God. Psalm 133 only has three verses and seventy five words but contains profound wisdom as it relates to the spirit of unity. As we discuss the principle of unity, I will use the proper expression of "God" who is the one true God, to refer to the God of Abraham, Isaac and Jacob, who is Yehovah our Elohim, the (LORD our God).

King David was a man after God's heart and wrote this Psalm thousands of years ago, but the verses of scripture in Psalm 133 are as important today as they were when it was written. Many ministers and students of the Bible have read and preached this Psalm over the years and have been blessed by the words of King David as it relates to unity.

The question that needs to be asked is, "Do we really grasp the understanding and importance of unity in our relationships, and most importantly the Body of Christ?" Before we go deeper into this study and examine unity, it would be wise to expound upon this Psalm and get the revelation that God gave to David as it relates to the anointing and blessing that is released upon us, when we walk together in perfect unity.

As I studied Psalm 133, one of the questions that was in my heart was, "Why did David write this Psalm and what was his intent?" Well we do know that David was a man after God's heart according to Acts 13:22. Now if David had the heart of God, everything that he wrote in the Psalms was to exalt, glorify and magnify the LORD. The very first thing that we read in Psalm 133: 1 is:

"A Song of degrees of David. Behold, how good and how pleasant it is for brethren to dwell together in unity!"

Many times when people read the Psalms in the King James Version, they will skip over the beginning or first part of the scripture. The very first thing that is written is: "A Song of degrees of David." When I first read this the understanding was unclear and there are many commentaries and explanations of it. Nevertheless, my understanding of the word "degrees" in the English language is something that is attained educationally, or the degrees of a thermostat. *The New Strong's Exhaustive Concordance of the Bible* gives us greater understanding. Degree's in the Hebrew is ma'ălâh, which is pronounced mah-al-aw' which means elevation, or the act or journey to a higher place, figuratively a thought arising, or literally a step or grade mark.

It is also a journey to a higher place or specifically a climactic progression in things that come up, or go up high, as in degree, stair, step, or story. Many commentators suggest that the probable origin of this name is that many of the Psalms that begin with "A Song of Degrees" where sung by the people on the ascents or going up to Jerusalem to attend the three great festivals.

So my understanding is that this Psalm of David represents a going up to a higher place, or prophetically an elevation in thought. Of course there are many other explanations for this, but could David in this particular Psalm be expressing the importance of unity or elevation in thought as the people journeyed to Jerusalem?

During the time of the feasts it was a time of rejoicing, unity, love for God, and one another as they journeyed to Jerusalem to worship, and to sacrifice to the Most High God. I believe this to be true! Because immediately after that he says, "Behold, how good and how pleasant it is for brethren to dwell together in unity!"

Let us pause for a moment. Selah. This is a profound statement. Is it not important that we ascend in thought and deed as it relates to unity? Should not the Body of Christ be journeying to a higher place as it relates to unity? If unity is a profound virtue and doctrine that the Bible exhorts us to embrace, why do we descend and not ascend in relation to it? Why do we disregard it, rather than acknowledge it? Why is the Body of Christ so divided on the important doctrines of interpretation? Should not the doctrines that are the most important be what unite our hearts together in Christ?

The doctrines that I am referring to are the virgin birth of Christ, the trinity, the blood of Jesus that was shed for our sins, Jesus deity as God, the resurrection, the authority and inerrancy of the scriptures, and his second coming and return. These are the most important doctrines that should unite our hearts together. It is not race, creed or color, and it certainly is not your denominational stance.

Although denominations have been around for hundreds of years, the first church in the book of Acts was not divided but unified as they preached the Gospel of the Kingdom, and they experienced unprecedented power by the Holy Spirit. If you can recall in the book of Revelation chapter 5, Jesus tells John the following:

"After these things I looked, and behold, a door standing open in heaven. And the first voice which I heard was like a trumpet speaking with me, saying, "Come up here, and I will show you things which must take place after this."
Revelation 4:1 NKJV

Notice there was ascension or a going up to a higher place where the LORD was. Was it not possible for the LORD to give John revelation down there? Of course, but instead he said, "Come up here, and I will show you the things that must take place." In Revelation 4: verse 2, John says, "Immediately I was in the Spirit; and behold, a throne set in heaven, and One sat on the throne." So in other words, the LORD said to come up here, which indicates a coming up to place, or higher where John would hear what the LORD had to say to him.

I do not want to engage in eisegesis, which is the process of interpreting a text or portion of text that introduces one's own presuppositions, agendas, or biases into the text. But the revelation of this is to profound to miss. He had to come up here, or higher where the LORD was to get the end time dispensation and revelation of things that were to come.

Does not going up higher indicate a place in the spirit where we can commune with the Most High. We must admit that the spiritual things of God are not the lower things of the earth which are fleshly. I find it very interesting that the LORD said come up here, rather than to speak to John down there in the earth realm!

In Psalm 133 verse 1, after it says a "Song of Degrees of David, it says, "Behold, how good and how pleasant it is when brethren dwell together in unity." Behold in the dictionary means to look upon, gaze or observe. In other words, look at this because it is something that deserves our attention.

He then goes on to say. "How good and how pleasant it is when brethren (an endearing term for brothers) dwell together in unity." Anyone who has been married for any length of time will confirm that it is indeed good and pleasant when there is unity in your household. Any Pastor or church leader will affirm this as well, that it is good and pleasant when the leadership and membership are unified.

Any military leader will attest that it is good and pleasant when there is good order and discipline when the troops are unified. Any athlete who engages in a team sport will agree that where there is unity, it is good and pleasant. Why? Because where there is unity we can accomplish much. Anything less than unity is division which is of a lower nature and consequently a work of the flesh.

There is no good thing in the flesh and there is no good thing in division. In Revelation 4: 1-2, it wasn't that God could not give John the understanding down there, but God said, "Come up here." In other words, what I am about to reveal to you can only be released to you when you come up here, to a higher place in the spirit where I can release this revelation to you. In other words it takes a higher degree of understanding that you cannot obtain down there! (Selah)

The Bible then says the following about John after he ascended up there to the place where the LORD was:

"And immediately I was in the spirit: and, behold, a throne was set in heaven, and one sat on the throne." Revelation 4:2 KJV

Did you get that? After he went up there where the LORD was, immediately he was in the spirit! Wow! The revelation is, we cannot do anything significant for the LORD when we have the mindset of the flesh which is of a lower nature. We must come up here, which is where? In the spirit where we can hear clearly from the LORD. The problem with many churches and leaders today is that they operate from down there, rather than coming up higher to walk in unity.

The flesh always produces a spirit of pride, selfishness, competition, self-righteousness, and a spirit of ownership. What is a spirit of ownership? That what we have achieved as it relates to the church belongs to us! This could be further from the truth! Did not Jesus say in Matthew 16:18, "Upon this rock I will build my church; and the gates of hell shall not prevail against it." Did not the LORD say, "My house shall be called the house of prayer; but you have made it a den of thieves." (Matt 21: 13, Mark 11: 17, Luke 19: 46)

So if it is God's church and God's house, we must do what the owner of the house desires and that is to build it upon the principles of unity!

How many of us know that we must walk in the spirit according to Gal 5: 16, we must live in the spirit according to Gal 5: 25, and be led by the spirit according to Rom 8: 14. Unity is a spiritual principle. It is not a fleshly principle. David said that it is good and pleasant when brothers and sisters dwell together in unity. So the question is, "If it is good and pleasant, why do we not engage in it more often?"

Although the LORD has blessed us as a body of believers in our organizations and denominations, the Body of Christ is not as unified as we could be. Yes, I agree there are organizations in the Body of Christ that have unity, and there are churches that practice unity, but overall there is a seed of division that separates the church by doctrine and race.

I do not want to go down that rabbit trail, but no man is an island, and we are not to be lone rangers in the Body of Christ. Although we are blessed and we are doing great things for the LORD, can you imagine the power that would be released if we unified as it relates to the LORD's Kingdom agenda?

For the Body of Christ, unity is the very essence of God. We find in the Bible that the Godhead of the Father, Son and Holy Spirit are unified in purpose. As a matter of fact one of the greatest prayers that many Messianic Jews and even believers pray is called the "Shema" found in the book of Deuteronomy 6: 4 which reads:

"Hear, O Israel: The LORD our God is one LORD."
Deuteronomy 6:4 KJV

We will discuss this more in detail later, but David says in Psalm 133 verse 2, that unity can be compared to that precious ointment upon the head, that ran down upon the beard, even Aaron's beard, that went down to the skirts of his garments.

"It is like the precious ointment upon the head that ran down upon the beard, even Aaron's beard: that went down to the skirts of his garments."
Psalms 133:2 KJV

What is that ointment? It is none other than the precious oil in Exodus 30: 23 which was given to

Moses by the LORD. The scriptures are listed in two translations to give you the proper understanding.

Exodus 30:22-25 KJV
22 Moreover the LORD spake unto Moses, saying,
23 Take thou also unto thee principal spices, of pure myrrh five hundred shekels, and of sweet cinnamon half so much, even two hundred and fifty shekels, and of sweet calamus two hundred and fifty shekels,
24 And of cassia five hundred shekels, after the shekel of the sanctuary, and of oil olive an hin:
25 And thou shalt make it an oil of holy ointment, an ointment compound after the art of the apothecary: it shall be an holy anointing oil.

Exodus 30:22-25 NKJV
22 Moreover the LORD spoke to Moses, saying:
23 "Also take for yourself quality spices--five hundred shekels of liquid myrrh, half as much sweet-smelling cinnamon (two hundred and fifty shekels), two hundred and fifty shekels of sweet-smelling cane,
24 five hundred shekels of cassia, according to the shekel of the sanctuary, and a hin of olive oil.
25 And you shall make from these a holy anointing oil, an ointment compounded according to the art of the perfumer. It shall be a holy anointing oil.

So the composition of this holy anointing oil was composed of sweet cinnamon, sweet calamus (sweet smelling cane), cassia, and olive oil. Adam Clarkes Commentary on the Bible states, "If anyone has ever smelled the odor of this holy anointing oil, it is very agreeable, and serves as a metaphor to point out the exquisite excellence of brotherly love."

So David is saying that unity can be compared to that precious heavenly anointing ointment or oil that was given to Moses by God himself. The smell is good and pleasant. It is very delightful and fills the room when it is applied. There is no odor in my opinion that is sweeter and delightful to smell! When we contrast the oil with unity, God says that it is good and pleasant!

The holy anointing oil was given by God to Moses for the service and use of the priests. In the times of the priesthood it was used to anoint the priests, Kings and the articles of the Tabernacle. It was even commanded in the Old Covenant that no one should use it for anything other than the service of the priesthood, and no other should copy this splendid recipe for the oil.

Exodus 30:31-33 NKJV
31 "And you shall speak to the children of Israel, saying: 'This shall be a holy anointing oil to Me throughout your generations.
32 It shall not be poured on man's flesh; nor shall you make any other like it, according to its composition. It is holy, and it shall be holy to you.
33 Whoever compounds any like it, or whoever puts any of it on an outsider, shall be cut off from his people."

So when David compares unity to the holy anointing oil, it is a splendid comparison indeed. David goes on to say in Psalms 133: 2, that it is like the precious oil upon the head, running down the beard, and down on the garments of Aaron the High Priest.

Now get a picture of this. If the holy anointing oil given by God is precious, splendid, delightful, good and pleasant, so is the unity among the brothers and sisters. Oils runs down and we shall see in the last verse that even as the oil runs down, blessings run down or come down upon all those that engage in it.

Verse 3 is even more profound. David says that unity is like the dew of Hermon descending upon the mountains of Zion. What exactly is the dew of Hermon? In order to get the proper understanding we must look to the King James interpretation for verse 3.

"As the dew of Hermon, and as the dew that descended upon the mountains of Zion: for there the LORD commanded the blessing, even life for evermore."
Psalms 133:3 KJV

There are different translations that give us unique illustrations of the dew of Hermon and the dew that descends upon the mountains of Zion. But the best understating in commentary that I have obtained comes from a commentary in *Useful Bible Studies* by Keith Simons:

"David in Psalm 133 is emphasizing the love that the people of God show for one another as it relates to unity. He then mentions Mount Hermon which is the tallest mountain in the entire region around 9,000 feet above sea level. It was in the north of the country that David ruled. Hermon is well-known for its dew (the water that gathers on the ground overnight). There is always plentiful water there. Jerusalem, including Zion where God's house stood, is in a dry region around 2,000 feet above sea level.

In other words, as there are two mountains, there are two or more people. God's dew, or God's blessings will fall upon those that engage in unity and are joined together in unity. Just as there are two mountains, one mountain, Hermon which has plentiful dew and Mount Zion which is dry. That means that the dew which is upon the higher mountain descends upon the lower mountain. So when we practice the principle and virtue of unity, like the dew it is plentiful, good, and pleasant and will flow down and cover Mount Zion.

As we can see, there is a blessing that is commanded upon those that are unified in love and fellowship. What David is saying is that just as the dew of God falls upon Mount Hermon and flows down to Mount Zion. It will also fall upon his people that are unified, and God will command the blessing, even life forevermore!

David is practically giving us a nugget of revelation that if we engage in unity, and practice this good and pleasant principle. God will command his blessing, even life forevermore. We may be dry in some areas of our life, we may not be experiencing his abundant blessings, but if we will follow unity and practice this principle, a blessing will be commanded upon each and every one of us!

Some of us may say, well I am already blessed, but can you imagine if the true church, the ecclesia would practice the principle that David describes, how great the blessing would be that descends upon us all. Sometimes we think that because are doing well, everything is good, and we have no lack, that we have arrived. Yet, God desires to bless his entire body, not just a few denominations, organizations, churches and local communities of Christ.

What has happened is that although we have been divided by denomination or race, God in his great grace has blessed us. There are so many churches all over America that have been established because of the call of God, but what would happen if we practiced unity and reached out to the church down the street, up the street or in another part of town.

Yes, we are indeed blessed by grace and mercy, but not because of unity in the entire body. We may have unity in some local communities of Christ, which is awesome, but what about those that are divided by interpretation and denomination. If we want to see the blessing commanded and even life forevermore by the LORD, it would behoove us to embrace this doctrinal principle of unity that King David gives us in Psalm 133.

CHAPTER 2

WHY IS UNITY IMPORTANT?

According to Psalm 133, the LORD commands the
blessing where there is a spirit of unity. Now if God
commands the blessing where there is unity,
shouldn't we endeavor to practice it in our families,
relationships and even in our churches? Brothers and
Sisters listen to the words of the Apostle Paul who
said in 2 Cor 2:11, "Lest Satan should get an
advantage of us: for we are not ignorant of his
devices."

Let me say that again. We are not ignorant of his
devices. Do you not know that the devices of Satan
are division, disunity, discord, dissension? Of course
we know this, but because of ignorance we ignore
what the Bible says, therefore we reap what we sow.

Now we do understand that we cannot practice unity
with everyone. There is a word called ecumenism
which is defined as the principle or aim of promoting
unity among the world's Christian Churches. There is
another definition that defines it as "a movement that
promotes worldwide unity among all religions
through greater cooperation."

When we look at these two definitions I would agree
that the aim of promoting unity among the world's
Christian churches is good if the doctrines of the faith
are in agreement as it relates to scripture, and the

LORD Jesus Christ.
I cannot and will not agree with any movement in which our doctrines and belief principles are not the same because the Bible says:

Can two walk together, except they be agreed?
Amos 3:3 KJV

According to GotQuestions.org as it relates to ecumenism, the writer states we should be involved in ecumenical cooperation with other Christian churches and other groups of believers if there is no doctrinal compromise on core Christian beliefs. If the gospel is not being watered-down or sidelined, if believers can maintain a clear testimony before the world, and if God is glorified, then we may freely and joyfully join with other believers in pursuit of God's kingdom."

In other words it is good to unify with others that have the same Biblical mindset and doctrinal stance. But if there is no agreement on the fundamental doctrines of the faith, there can be no compromise. The Apostle Paul rebuked the church at Galatia because of this.

Galatians 1:8-9 KJV
8 But though we, or an angel from heaven, preach any other gospel unto you than that which we have preached unto you, let him be accursed.
9 As we said before, so say I now again, If any man preach any other gospel unto you than that ye have

received, let him be accursed.

Now there are some that may disagree with me, but the scripture says:

2 Corinthians 6:14-16 KJV
14 Be ye not unequally yoked together with unbelievers: for what fellowship hath righteousness with unrighteousness and what communion hath light with darkness?
15 And what concord hath Christ with Belial? or what part hath he that believeth with an infidel?
16 And what agreement hath the temple of God with idols? for ye are the temple of the living God; as God hath said, I will dwell in them, and walk in them; and I will be their God, and they shall be my people.

The key word in coming together in unity is agreement. Because when we are in agreement, we have something in common. When we are in agreement and have a common goal, it is easier to work together. We will discuss the principles of agreement in more detail later.

The Bible contains some great teachings on unity. Even Jesus taught principles on unity and it is evident when he bought twelve unlearned men together as Disciples. He taught them, empowered them, rebuked them, and poured into them over a three year period and then they became Apostles. They were then empowered with the Holy Spirit on the day of Pentecost and went all over the region preaching the Gospel of the Kingdom. As a result the church was birthed according to Acts 11: 26.

"And when he had found him, he brought him unto Antioch. And it came to pass, that a whole year they assembled themselves with the church, and taught much people. And the disciples were called Christians first in Antioch."
Acts 11:26 KJV

I believe that the church's ability to reach the lost, bring in the end time harvest, and to preach and teach the Gospel of Jesus Christ effectively we must have a foundation of unity. How can we reach a lost world for Jesus Christ and we are not unified.

It is hypocritical to think that simply because we are the church that people will embrace us. As a matter of fact, the opposite may be true. Many millennials and young people are not embracing the Church in these last days! Now don't get me wrong there are some young people who love the LORD, have great potential, and are making an eternal difference for the Kingdom of God. Yet, there are just as many that are not embracing the Church. Could it be that they see hypocrisy, and that we are not practicing all that we are preaching?

Unity comes from the root word UNIT, which is defined as: "Any one of several parts that make up a whole part, or any measurement that there is one of." The LORD gave me an acronym that I would like to share as it relates to a unit. UNIT - "YoU iN I Together" which is translated you and I together equals one.

Solomon's Wisdom on Unity

Solomon gives us some wisdom as it relates to unity and oneness in the book of Ecclesiastes as well. Many times we read these scriptures but do we really grasp the significance of them?

Ecclesiastes 4:9-12 KJV
9 **Two are better than one**; because they have a good reward for their labor.
10 For if they fall, the one will lift up his fellow: but woe to him that is alone when he falls; for he has not another to help him up.
11 Again, if two lie together, then they have heat: but how can one be warm alone?
12 And if one prevail against him, two shall withstand him; and a threefold cord is not quickly broken.

Solomon in his wisdom said that two are better than one. Why? Because they have a good reward for their labor! The Bible says that if one falls, the other one will lift him up. It also says woe to him that falls, and has no one to lift him up. It also says that two persons together provide heat, but how can one be warm alone?

25

Verse 12 goes even further by saying it may be easy to overtake or overpower one person. But it is hard to prevail against two people, and a threefold cord is not quickly broken.

These are very profound scriptures that Solomon gives us concerning the power of one. The wisdom presented here shows us that when there one person alone, there is not much power. But when there are two or three people working together toward a common goal, there is greater power to accomplish the purpose.

We have read these scriptures for years, but do we really understand the profoundness of what Solomon the wise man is saying? Solomon is saying that two or more people united together as one is a great benefit. Why? Because they have more power, and can accomplish more together than when they are alone. He that has an ear to hear let him hear!

Jesus Speaks on Unity and Division

In Luke chapter 11, something interesting happens. Jesus is performing deliverance and casting out a devil. The people that witness it believe that he cast out the devil by the spirit of Beelzebub, who is the chief or ruler of demons or devils.

Luke 11:14-15 NKJV
14 And He was casting out a demon, and it was mute. So it was, when the demon had gone out, that the

mute spoke; and the multitudes marveled.
15 But some of them said, "He casts out demons by
Beelzebub, the ruler of the demons."

Jesus being a prophet knew their thoughts and gave
them some profound wisdom on deliverance. Not
only did he give them wisdom on deliverance, but he
shattered their ignorance, and then gave them some
great wisdom on unity and division.

Luke 11:17-19 NKJV
17 But He, knowing their thoughts, said to them:
"Every kingdom divided against itself is brought to
desolation, and a house divided against a house falls.
18 If Satan also is divided against himself, how will
his kingdom stand? Because you say I cast out
demons by Beelzebub.
19 And if I cast out demons by Beelzebub, by whom
do your sons cast them out? Therefore they will be
your judges.

Jesus said every kingdom divided against itself is
brought to desolation. Desolation means complete
destruction and emptiness. He also said that a house
divided against itself cannot stand. In other words
division brings desolation and destruction, and it
cannot stand strong. People of God, let us think
about this for a moment. Tell me how can any
kingdom stand if they are in division? Now don't
miss the wisdom in this passage of scripture. If a
kingdom is divided against itself and there is no
unity, it will not stand. If a house is divided against

itself, it will not stand.

Jesus has just given us the most profound teaching in a few passages of scripture that would greatly benefit us if we were not only hearers but doers of the Word. If we applied the principle of unity to our churches, marriages, families, and any endeavors that we desire to pursue we would have much more power to succeed in the purposes of God! Now contrast that with division. If there is division and desolation, destruction is not far behind!

He then turns his attention to spiritual warfare and says in verse 18, If Satan is divided against himself, how will his kingdom stand?

"If Satan also be divided against himself, how shall his kingdom stand? Because ye say that I cast out devils through Beelzebub."
Luke 11:18 KJV

Jesus was literally saying that if I am on Satan and Beelzebub's side, why would I cast out the demon? Jesus said it doesn't make sense. If I was on the devils side why would I cast out a member of my own team? Because then I would go against the team!

Jesus is giving wisdom on spiritual warfare and as a bonus gives them some teaching on unity and division. Jesus said I am not on the devils side! As a matter of fact I came to set the captives free! This is evident in Luke chapter 4 after Jesus was anointed and empowered with the Holy Spirit.

Luke 4:18 KJV
18 The Spirit of the Lord is upon me, because he hath anointed me to preach the gospel to the poor; he hath sent me to heal the brokenhearted, to preach deliverance to the captives, and recovering of sight to the blind, to set at liberty them that are bruised.

Jesus goes on to say in verse 19 that if I, the Son of Man, and Son of God cast out demons by another spirit. Then by what spirit do your sons cast them out, because they will be their judges. Jesus is literally saying that if I cast out demons by Beelzebub, which is definitely not true. Than by what spirit do your sons cast them out, for they will be their judges.

Jesus was making a point using spiritual sarcasm to show them their ignorance as it relates to spiritual warfare and division. How many of us know that when we engage in spiritual warfare, it is essential that we be on one accord? Jesus then continues to expound on spiritual warfare.

Luke 11:20-23 KJV
20 But if I with the finger of God cast out devils, no doubt the kingdom of God is come upon you.
21 When a strong man armed keeps his palace, his goods are in peace:
22 But when a stronger than he shall come upon him, and overcome him, he taketh from him all his

armor wherein he trusted, and divides his spoils.
23 He that is not with me is against me: and he that gathers not with me scatters.

The LORD than tells them that if I am casting out devils by the finger of God, know for a surety that the kingdom of God has come upon you. He then gives us the wisdom of spiritual warfare in binding the strong man that comes to kill, steal and destroy in verse 21-22. The strong man, demon or evil spirit must be bound, or rendered powerless and cast out. To bind means to tie up. So the enemy must be tied or bound where he can do no harm.

How many of us know that one can put a thousand to flight and two can put ten thousand to flight? (Deut 32: 30) There is definitely strength in unity! Verse 23 is even more profound! Jesus said, "He that is not with me is against me, and he that does not gather with me scatters!"

Did you get that? Jesus said if you are not united with me, you are against me. If you are not gathering with me, you are scattering.

People of God, we should be united in our battle against the wicked one. Team Jesus Christ is not divided. We should be unified. Yet, there are people and churches all over the country that are scattering. It does not matter what race, creed, color or denomination you are! The Kingdom of God must be unified in preaching the true Gospel of the Kingdom.

If we are not unified in this purpose, the root of division and pride will eventually hurt and hinder us.

CHAPTER 3

TWO SOLID FOUNDATIONS: UNITY AND LOVE

Matthew 7:24-27 KJV
24 Therefore whosoever hears these sayings of mine, and does them, I will liken him unto a wise man, which built his house upon a rock:
25 And the rain descended, and the floods came, and the winds blew, and beat upon that house and it fell not: for it was founded upon a rock.
26 And every one that hears these sayings of mine, and does them not, shall be likened unto a foolish man, which built his house upon the sand:
27 And the rain descended, and the floods came, and the winds blew, and beat upon that house; and it fell: and great was the fall of it.

How many of us know that the foundations of unity and love are strong foundations? Unity is an important virtue and principle in the Bible. (Read Psalm 133: 1)

"A Song of degrees of David. Behold, how good and how pleasant it is for brethren to dwell together in unity!"
Psalms 133:1 KJV

Love is an even great principle and virtue. (Read John 13: 34)

"A new commandment I give unto you, That ye love

one another; as I have loved you, that ye also love one another."
John 13:34 KJV

When we operate and build upon these two solid foundations there is nothing that we cannot achieve in Jesus name!

Let us look to the scriptures as it relates to building on a solid foundation in Christ. In Matt 7: 24-27, Jesus gives us some wisdom as it relates hearing his Word and doing it. He compares it to building on either a solid or sandy foundation. Let's take a look.

Two homes are built, one on the rock and the other on sand. There are two builders, one is wise the other foolish. They have the same circumstances. Violent storms which include rain, floods and wind. Yet there are different results. One stands firm and one collapses.

Why? The difference is the foundation. Are you building your house on the principles of unity and love which will cause us to stand, or division and disunity which will cause us to fall?

Do you ever notice that Jesus often said, "He that has an ear, let him hear?" The reason why Jesus said this is because he was saying something so profound that it was worth listening too. The problem is that there are way to many hearers and enough doers of the Word.

This is where the problem begins in the Body of Christ. We love the Word of God and we love good preaching and teaching, but oftentimes the doing gets lost in the message. The hearing of the Word should give way to the doing of the Word. James said something profound in the book of James chapter 1:

James 1:22-25 KJV

22 But be ye doers of the word, and not hearers only, deceiving your own selves.

23 For if any be a hearer of the word, and not a doer, he is like unto a man beholding his natural face in a glass:

24 For he beholds himself, and goes his way, and straightway forgets what manner of man he was.

25 But whoso looks into the perfect law of liberty, and continues therein, he being not a forgetful hearer, but a doer of the work, this man shall be blessed in his deed.

According to James, if we are hearers of the Word only and not doers we are deceived. The blessing is in the hearing and doing of Word. So let us pause for a moment and consider this. There are many people in the body of Christ that love the LORD, love the Word and love God's people, but they are deceived. How can we read such profound scriptures and yet not take heed of what the Bible says concerning unity in the Body of Christ!

We must remember that the foundation of unity will cause us to stand strong. The foundation of division will bring desolation and destruction.

Let's take a look at Matthew 7:24-27 KJV
24 Therefore whosoever hears these sayings of mine, and does them, I will liken him unto a wise man, which built his house upon a rock:
25 And the rain descended, and the floods came, and the winds blew, and beat upon that house and it fell not: for it was founded upon a rock.
26 And every one that hears these sayings of mine, and does them not, shall be likened unto a foolish man, which built his house upon the sand:
27 And the rain descended, and the floods came, and the winds blew, and beat upon that house; and it fell: and great was the fall of it.

Jesus said in verse 24, whoever hears these sayings of mine and does them, I will liken or compare him to a wise man which built his house on the rock. This is interesting. The LORD is giving us wisdom that if we take heed to the words that he gives us and we are doers of the Word, we are wise men and women of God who build upon a rock, which is a solid foundation.

"Therefore whosoever hears these sayings of mine, and doeth them, I will liken him unto a wise man, which built his house upon a rock."
Matthew 7:24 KJV

Despite the heavy rain, floods, and wind that beat on that house it did not fall. Why? Because it was founded or built on a solid foundation. Jesus then makes another comparison in Matt 7: 26-27:

26 And every one that hears these sayings of mine, and does them not, shall be likened unto a foolish man, which built his house upon the sand:
27 And the rain descended, and the floods came, and the winds blew, and beat upon that house; and it fell: and great was the fall of it.

This is an amazing parable told by the LORD concerning two foundations. One built on a rock is built on the sayings and doing of the Word. The other one built on sand which is the hearing and not doing of the Word. The rain, flood and winds are the trials, tribulations, troubles, tests and temptations of life. When these things come upon us, how you stand is dependent upon how you hear the sayings of Jesus and do them.

Our goal and desire should always be hearers and doers of the Word of God. Everything that Jesus taught us in the Bible is profound wisdom for life. Jesus even said in John 6: 63:

"It is the Spirit who gives life; the flesh profits nothing. The words that I speak to you are spirit, and they are life."
John 6:63 NKJV

Now if his Words are spirit and life and will cause us to stand in the midst of any storm, shouldn't we apply it to our lives? The solid foundations of unity and love will cause us to stand strong in the midst of division, discord, disunity and dissension. Yet we fail many times because we have not heeded the words of our blessed Savior!

Before Jesus ascended into heaven, John records a powerful prayer that Jesus prayed in John chapter 17: 1-23. Jesus prayed a very profound prayer that I believe was a guiding principle for the people of God. Let's take a look at this profound prayer.

John 17:20-23 NKJV
20 "I do not pray for these alone, but also for those who will believe in Me through their word;
21 **that they all may be one,** as You, Father, are in Me, and I in You; **that they also may be one in Us,** that the world may believe that You sent Me.
22 And the glory which You gave Me I have given them, **that they may be one just as We are one:**
23 I in them, and You in Me; **that they may be made perfect in one**, and that the world may know that You have sent Me, and have loved them as You have loved Me.

This is one of the most powerful prayers that are recorded in scripture for the believers. Jesus prayed that we would be as one four times. Now we know that every word shall be established by the testimony of two or three witnesses, because three is a divine and perfect number. Just as the Godhead is perfect as one, so should we be perfect as one.

"Hear, O Israel: The LORD our God, the LORD is one!"
Deuteronomy 6:4 NKJV

Unity on the Day of Pentecost

Acts 2:1-4 NKJV
1 When the Day of Pentecost had fully come, they were **all with one accord in one place**.
2 And suddenly there came a sound from heaven, as of a rushing mighty wind, and it filled the whole house where they were sitting.
3 Then there appeared to them divided tongues, as of fire, and one sat upon each of them.
4 And they were all filled with the Holy Spirit and began to speak with other tongues, as the Spirit gave them utterance.

Notice that the disciples were together on one accord on the Day of Pentecost. They all had the same mind and same spirit as they waited for the promise of the spirit spoken by Jesus. One of the things I have found in relation to revelational Bible study is to study every name, word, number, and place. The key word in Acts 2 verse 1 is they were all **on one accord in one place**. Herein lies the revelation of a powerful, victorious church! Being on accord in one place!

After the Holy Spirit was poured upon the Apostles, they were endued with power from on high. (Acts 2:

1-4) Peter than began to preach with power in Acts 2: 38-40 and exhorted the people saying:

Acts 2:38-40 NKJV
38 Then Peter said to them, "Repent, and let every one of you be baptized in the name of Jesus Christ for the remission of sins; and you shall receive the gift of the Holy Spirit.
39 For the promise is to you and to your children, and to all who are afar off, as many as the Lord our God will call."
40 And with many other words he testified and exhorted them, saying, "Be saved from this perverse generation."

The Bible says that as a result of Peter's powerful preaching by the Holy Spirit, the following happened:

"Then those who gladly received his word were baptized; and that day about three thousand souls were added to them."
Acts 2:41 NKJV

Isn't it amazing that after the Apostles were gathered together on one accord, the Holy Spirit came upon them and a manifestation of power was released them. It was so powerful that a spirit of unity and love was manifested in the lives of every person that believed on the LORD Jesus Christ.

When we read Acts 2: 42-47, we find one of the most powerful passages of scripture concerning unity and love. This is why the Psalmist David prophetically proclaimed in Psalm 133: 1, "How good and how pleasant it is when brethren dwell together in unity." Let's take a look:

Acts 2:42-47 NKJV

42 And they continued steadfastly in the apostles' doctrine and fellowship, in the breaking of bread, and in prayers.

43 Then fear came upon every soul, and many wonders and signs were done through the apostles.

44 Now all who believed were together, and had all things in common,

45 and sold their possessions and goods, and divided them among all, as anyone had need.

46 So continuing daily with one accord in the temple, and breaking bread from house to house, they ate their food with gladness and simplicity of heart,

47 praising God and having favor with all the people. And the Lord added to the church daily those who were being saved.

The Bible says that they continued steadfastly in the Apostles doctrine, fellowship, breaking of bread and prayers. The Bible says that all who believed were together and had all things common. (Verse 44) Not only that but they began to sell possessions and goods and gave to everyone in need. (Verse 45) Now you know that this was truly a work of the spirit, because no one sells their possessions and goods and gives them away!

Verse 46 says that they continued with one accord, breaking bread, fellowshipping, praising God, having favor and God added to the church daily those that were being saved! This is truly a wonderful example of what the church should be doing today! The important principle that enabled the first century church to be successful in coming together was the principle of unity.

Unity in the Body of Christ

The Apostle Paul also spoke about the importance of unity in Ephesians chapter 4, verses 1-7. Let's take a look:

Ephesians 4:1-7 NKJV
1 I, therefore, the prisoner of the Lord, beseech you to walk worthy of the calling with which you were called,
2 with all lowliness and gentleness, with longsuffering, bearing with one another in love,
3 endeavoring to keep the unity of the Spirit in the bond of peace.
4 There is one body and one Spirit, just as you were called in one hope of your calling;
5 one Lord, one faith, one baptism;
6 one God and Father of all, who is above all and through all, and in you all.

Paul speaking to the Church at Ephesus while in a prison cell told the Saints in verse 1, "I beseech, admonish, or plead with you to walk worthy of the calling with which you are called." He went on to say in verse 2-3, with all lowliness, gentleness, and longsuffering, **bearing with each other in love, endeavoring to keep the spirit of unity in the bond of peace.**

Did you get that? He mentions the two foundations that are important for the church; Love and Unity. Not only that but we should endeavor to keep the unity of the Spirit in the bond of peace. Endeavoring means to use speed, be prompt, earnest, and diligent in keeping the unity of the Spirit in the bond of peace. In other words do everything possible to make sure that you follow this. Why did Paul say this?

Paul knew that it was so important that the Body of Christ be on one accord and not divided. He said we should do everything possible to follow this principle. Why? Verse 4-6 answers it. There is one body and one Spirit. There is one Lord, one faith, one baptism and one God and Father of all, who is above all, through all and in you all.

In other words the Body of Christ is one body. Although the Body of Christ is universal all over the world we are one in Jesus name. Although there are communities of Christ all over the United States we are one in Jesus Name! We cannot afford to miss that awesome principle that Paul speaks about. We should always bear with each other in love, endeavoring to keep the spirit of unity in the bond of peace.

One Body with Many Members

In a letter to the Corinthian church Paul again speaks about the body being unified. Let's read:

1 Corinthians 12:12-31 NKJV
12 For as the body is one and has many members, but all the members of that one body, being many, are one body, so also is Christ.
13 For by one Spirit we were all baptized into one body--whether Jews or Greeks, whether slaves or free--and have all been made to drink into one Spirit.
14 For in fact the body is not one member but many.
15 If the foot should say, "Because I am not a hand, I am not of the body," is it therefore not of the body?
16 And if the ear should say, "Because I am not an eye, I am not of the body," is it therefore not of the body?
17 If the whole body were an eye, where would be the hearing? If the whole were hearing, where would be the smelling?
18 But now God has set the members, each one of them, in the body just as He pleased.
19 And if they were all one member, where would the body be?
20 But now indeed there are many members, yet one body.
21 And the eye cannot say to the hand, "I have no need of you"; nor again the head to the feet, "I have no need of you."
22 No, much rather, those members of the body

which seem to be weaker are necessary.

23 And those members of the body which we think to be less honorable, on these we bestow greater honor; and our unpresentable parts have greater modesty,

24 but our presentable parts have no need. But God composed the body, having given greater honor to that part which lacks it,

25 that there should be no schism in the body, but that the members should have the same care for one another.

26 And if one member suffers, all the members suffer with it; or if one member is honored, all the members rejoice with it.

27 Now you are the body of Christ, and members individually.

1 Corinthians 12 is a wonderful exhortation from the Apostle Paul about the Body of Christ being one. Paul in verse 12 uses the example of a human body with many body parts that make up the human body. He goes on to say as the body has many parts but is still one body, so is the body of Christ. The body of Christ has many members worldwide, but we are still one body in Christ.

This is a wonderful example because although there are many members in the body of Christ, we are still one body. The body of Christ is not composed of many bodies, it is composed of many members. There is one body of believers regardless of what country we live in, or what church that we attend. Verse 14 says, "For the body is not one member, but many."

Now what is even more interesting is that Paul says in verse 18, "But now God has set the members, each one of them, in the body just as He pleased." Although we are one body of believers the church or ecclesia is made up of the universal body of Christ which is believers worldwide. There are many communities of Christ or local churches which compose of members of the Body of Christ. Paul says that God has set the members in the body as He desires.

So what is Paul saying? I believe that Paul is saying that regardless of the local church body we belong to, it is because God has ordained it or caused it to be. So regardless of where we may be fellowshipping or what denomination or organization we belong to. God has set us in that body as he has pleased. Now I am not referring to any church but I am referring to those churches that follow the Apostles doctrine (Acts 2: 42), the Gospel of our Lord Jesus Christ (Mark 1: 1) and the Gospel of the Kingdom (Matt 4: 23, Mark 1: 14-15)

Paul goes on to talk about the members of the body and how each part of the body is important and has a function.

1 Corinthians 12:20-22 NKJV
20 But now indeed there are many members, yet one body.

21 And the eye cannot say to the hand, "I have no need of you"; nor again the head to the feet, "I have no need of you."
22 No, much rather, those members of the body which seem to be weaker are necessary.

Paul again confirms in verse 20 that we are many members, yet one body. Verses 21-22 are important because Paul gives us an example of the human body in which the eye cannot say to the hand, "I have no need of you." Nor can the head say to the feet, "I have no need of you." In fact, the members of the body which seem to be weaker are necessary.

So how does this relate to the entire Body of Christ, the local communities of Christ, or the believers in Christ? Well there are mega churches, medium size churches small churches, and many members of those churches,
but each one has a part to play as it relates to the preaching and teaching of the Gospel of the Kingdom.

Each part of the body is important. No one church is better than another church. This is where we have missed it. If we read 1 Corinthians 12: 20-25 slowly, we will get the revelation that we have missed for many years.

Every bonafide Church is important. Every member of the body of Christ is important, and we all have a part to play. Yet for some reason we have this idea that because we are mega or smaller we are better. This is a mistake and very unwise. Every part of the body is important according to the Apostle Paul. Many times when we read this passage of scripture, we focus on the gifts of 1 Cor 12: 28-30, but we have missed it entirely.

This is not so much about the spiritual gifts which are important of course, but it much more a discourse on being united as one body of believers. If you read further in chapter 13, Paul goes into a discourse on the importance of love, which is one of the solid foundations we discussed earlier in this chapter.

Brothers and Sisters, we must remember one important thing; without love or unity we are nothing but noise and our spiritual gifts will fail according to 1 Cor 13: 1-8.

CHAPTER 4

Can you see what God Sees?

Mark 8:22-25 NKJV
22 Then He came to Bethsaida; and they brought a blind man to Him, and begged Him to touch him.
23 So He took the blind man by the hand and led him out of the town. And when He had spit on his eyes and put His hands on him, He asked him if he saw anything.
24 And he looked up and said, "I see men like trees, walking."
25 Then He put His hands on his eyes again and made him look up. And he was restored and saw everyone clearly.

How many of us know that it is important that we see as God sees? In other words we should have the mind of Christ. Paul said in Phil 2: 5, "Let this mind be in you which was also in Christ Jesus." It is so important that we as the Body of Christ be in the perfect will of God and desire to do the will of God. Jesus said in Matt 6: 10 that we should pray:

"Your kingdom come, your will be done in earth as it is in heaven."
Matthew 6:10 NKJV

Why should be pray this? Because we should be in total agreement with the Word of God, and we should pray that his perfect will be done in earth as it is in heaven. We should also pray that his perfect will be done in our lives. In other words we should have the heart of God as it relates to Kingdom business in Jesus name, and we must have the mind of Christ and eyes to see what God sees! Let me explain!

When we see what God sees, it will cause us to do what God would do and to say what God's Word says. Now some may say, "Pastor the church is at its finest hour, churches are growing, souls are being saved and everything appears to be alright." But I want you to know that God does not see as we see. The Bible says that man looks on the outer appearance but God looks at the heart. (1 Sam 16: 7). The Bible also says that what is highly esteemed in the sight of man is abomination in the sight of God. (Luke 16: 15)

Isaiah said in Isaiah 55: 8-9:
"For my thoughts are not your thoughts, neither are your ways my ways, saith the LORD. For as the heavens are higher than the earth, so are my ways higher than your ways, and my thoughts than your thoughts."
Isaiah 55:8-9 KJV

In these last days, it is becoming increasingly important that we not only have the mind of Christ, and spiritual ears to hear, but even more importantly spiritual eyes to see. There are many people today that may see in the natural but they have no idea what God is doing in the spiritual, because they don't have spiritual eyes to see what God sees.

In other words we need the eyes of our understanding opened that we may see spiritually and come into total agreement with God's Word as it relates to unity in the body of Christ. Maybe this is why David said in Psalm 119:18 "Open my eyes, that I may behold wondrous things in your law."

Why is it important to see what God sees? When we see what God sees, we see a world gone crazy, we see unsaved family, friends, co-workers, neighbors and people who need a Savior. We also see that in the midst of everything going on around us that Jesus is coming soon!

When we see like Christ, we have the understanding of Christ and we walk in unconditional love. We walk in obedience to the Word and practice unity, patience, humility, and compassion.

All throughout the Gospels, we find people running after Jesus, and running to Jesus. We don't find many people doing this today. Today people run everywhere but to the one who can make a way out of no way. People need to know that Jesus is the only way to get their healing.

They need to know that Jesus is the only way you can truly get a breakthrough. Jesus is the only way to get peace. Jesus is the only way to get strength in the midst of adversity and guess what? Jesus is the only way to walk in complete unity as a Body of Believers.

Jesus Causes a Blind Man to See Clearly

In Mark 8: 22-26, Jesus heals a blind man, but he didn't heal him the way he healed others! Let's take a look:

Mark 8:22-25
22 And he cometh to Bethsaida; and they bring a blind man unto him, and besought him to touch him.
23 And he took the blind man by the hand, and led him out of the town; and when he had spit on his eyes, and put his hands upon him, he asked him if he saw ought.
24 And he looked up, and said, I see men as trees, walking.
25 After that he put his hands again upon his eyes, and made him look up: and he was restored, and saw every man clearly.

The Bibles says that he came to Bethsaida and they brought a blind man to Jesus to be healed. What is interesting is that Jesus didn't heal him in the manner that he normally healed others. He took the man by the hand (verse 23) and led him out of town. Not only did he take him out of town, but he put some miracle spit on his eyes, laid his hands on him and asked him what he saw.

In verse 24, the blind man said, "I see men as trees walking." The Bible says in verse 25 that Jesus laid his hands upon him again and he was restored and saw every man clearly.

Do you know why Jesus led him out of town?
Because of the unbelief in Bethsaida. In the Gospel of Matthew we read about Bethsaida's unbelief.

Matthew 11:20-21 NKJV
20 Then He began to rebuke the cities in which most of His mighty works had been done, because they did not repent:
21 "Woe to you, Chorazin! Woe to you, Bethsaida! For if the mighty works which were done in you had been done in Tyre and Sidon, they would have repented long ago in sackcloth and ashes.

Not only did they have a spirit of unbelief, but they had spiritual blindness as well. 2 Cor 5: 7 says that we walk by faith and not by sight.

The Bible also says in Hebrews 11: 1, "Now faith is the substance of things hoped for, the evidence of things not seen." Jesus could do no mighty works there because of their unbelief. Could it be that the reason we don't see more miracles in the Body of Christ because of our unbelief?

When Jesus spit on the man's eyes and laid his hands on him he did not see clearly. Jesus had to lay his hands on the man a second time so that he could see. (Mark 8: 23-25)

How many of us know that there is some revelation in this story? Jesus led the man out of town to heal him because of the unbelief in that town. Unbelief is dangerous and can cause us to miss God. Unbelief is synonymous with spiritual blindness. Only through the eyes of faith can we see what God sees!

The revelation in this story is that sometimes we need God to open our eyes again to see what he sees. Many of us in the Body of Christ have been saved, we love the LORD, and we are even walking in purpose. But I believe we need the LORD to touch our eyes again as it relates to unity in the Body of Christ! Why? Because we don't see as clearly as we should see.

We live in a time where we must choose to trust God completely with the eyes of faith! Elijah told the people of God in 1 Kings 18:21:

"And Elijah came to all the people, and said, "How long will you falter between two opinions? If the LORD is God, follow Him; but if Baal, follow him." But the people answered him not a word."
1 Kings 18:21 NKJV

How long will be falter between two opinions as it relates to unity and division? If unity is of God, we should embrace it. If division is not of God we must denounce it.

Why is it that we know what the Bible says about unity, we talk about unity, but we don't always practice unity. As a matter of fact we are quite quiet on the subject!

If God's Word is true and we know it is, then follow after Jesus, and follow the principles of unity and love! If we can't see what God sees, then we need another touch from God to open our spiritual eyes! Jesus told the Church at Laodicea something interesting.

Revelation 3:17-19 NKJV
17 Because you say, 'I am rich, have become wealthy, and have need of nothing'--and do not know that you are wretched, miserable, poor, blind, and naked--
18 I counsel you to buy from Me gold refined in the fire, that you may be rich; and white garments, that you may be clothed, that the shame of your nakedness may not be revealed; and anoint your eyes with eye salve, that you may see.
19 As many as I love, I rebuke and chasten. Therefore be zealous and repent.

What is interesting is that this Church did not see as Jesus saw them which was lukewarm. They saw themselves as rich, wealthy, and had no need of anything. (Verse 16-17) Jesus saw them as wretched, miserable, poor, blind and naked. He even gave them some wise counsel in verse 18: "I counsel you to buy from Me gold refined in the fire, that you may be rich; and white garments, that you may be clothed, that the shame of your nakedness may not be revealed; **and anoint your eyes with eye salve, that you may see."**

Did you get that? They saw themselves a certain way, but God saw something quite different! They did not see what God saw, so he said you need to anoint your eyes with eye salve that you may see! People of God, this is such as profound word. We need eyes to see what God sees as it relates to Kingdom business. Many times we see things a certain way, but it may not be necessarily what God sees. We should follow the examples of scripture that exhort us to do the following:

Psalms 121:1-2 NKJV
1 A Song of Ascents. **I will lift up my eyes to the hills, from whence comes my help?**
2 My help comes from the LORD, Who made heaven and earth.

Hebrews 12:2 NKJV
2 looking unto Jesus, the author and finisher of our faith, who for the joy that was set before Him endured the cross, despising the shame, and has sat down at the right hand of the throne of God.

For many years we have seen things the way we have desired to see them, but as we see it is not always the way God sees. Our prayer should be that the LORD would touch our eyes again to see clearly the importance of corporate unity and love in the Body of Christ.

CHAPTER 5

The Power of Agreement and Unity

The message of unity is so important for the times because there is so much disorder in these last days that we live in. And where you find division and disunity you will also find disorder and confusion.

All over the world there are relationships, marriages, and families in disorder because of division, dissension and disunity. We even find that even churches are divided because they cannot agree. Now as a whole this is not the case because there are relationships, families, and churches that are unified and doing great things for the Kingdom of God.

Nevertheless, I find that there is a spirit of disagreement all over the country as it relates to politics, religion, gun control and even the family structure. I like to read the news on popular news outlets so that I can stay in touch with current events, but I don't like to read the comments of readers.

Why? Because many of those people are crude and rude, and everyone has a comment about something whether it be race, politics, guns, religion and the list goes on.

People are so divided on so many issues in this country that it is a shame, and it is quite the same in the church. Everyone has a third heaven revelation. Everyone believes that they are right and correct, and yet no one knows it all, and no one has all the answers except the Lord, and what he has revealed to us in his Word!

One thing I can say is that I believe that the Word of God is truth, because Jesus said in John 6:63, "It is the Spirit who gives life, the flesh profits nothing." The words that I speak to you are spirit and they are life. So if you really want the truth concerning wisdom and everything that pertains to your life, the bible has the answer!

Many people are in error because they lean on their own understanding and wisdom. God is all powerful and all-knowing and can give us clarity on life issues, especially as it relates to agreement and unity! One thing I want you to remember as we talk about the power of agreement and unity.

1. Agreement and unity is the key to blessing in your family, in the church, and in your life.

Let's define what agreement is: Agreement is the act of coming together as it relates to decisions and transactions. It is harmony of opinion, or it is a compatible arrangement between parties regarding a course of action. It is also a covenant. It is also the state of being of one opinion, in one accord or in harmony with one another! Amos 3:3 says, "Can two walk together except they be agreed?" How can marriages stay strong except the husband and wife agree? How can we as a church grow and do great work as it relates to the Kingdom of God except we agree? One of the reasons why people fight and argue is because of disagreement and disharmony, or one person's opinion over another person's opinion saying, "I'm right you're wrong, you're wrong, I'm right!"

This is why people get divorced, and the divorce papers say they had irreconcilable differences. Irreconcilable means they were not able to reconcile or agree. In other words they were not able to compromise, adjust or submit to one another. Another definition is one or two more conflicting ideas or beliefs that cannot be brought into harmony.

Even in the church we need to understand that we are all serving one Lord, one faith, and one baptism. One of the reasons we have so many denominations is because of interpretation. Because somebody didn't agree with someone else's interpretation of what they read or how they perceive or interpret it.

One reason churches break up and split is because of disagreement. I can recall there was an old Navy Chief that used to tell his sailors, "There are only three things you need to understand in relation to how we run things around here. There's the Navy's way, the Chief's way and the right way. There was no room for negotiation and disagreement. Even in the church we need to understand there is only one way we can do things, and that is God's way, and not man's way!

If we want to see the hand of God move with miracles in our churches and the body of Christ as a whole, we must get on one accord and not division, dissension, disunity, discord and disagreement. Can you imagine if the church got on one accord, I mean really got on one accord and came together what we could accomplish?

If we all pooled our resources together we could accomplish so much. But because we have the mentality of me, myself and I, me and my two that's all we gonna do, me and my three that's all its gonna me, me and my four and no more, we will never do great exploits and great things at it relates to the Kingdom of God!

Can you imagine if we all really came together, no one would lack, needs would be met, the church would overflow with excellence and we could take our communities, cities and country for Jesus Christ!

The Kingdom of Darkness is unified to Divide Us

As I was meditating on the Word some time ago, the LORD showed me that the Kingdom of Darkness works together to divide us. This sounds like an oxymoron or a conflicting statement but it is true.

The Kingdom of Darkness and its unholy host work together to divide us!

The Kingdom of God which includes the people of God are the light of the world! When we are unified we can do much damage to the Kingdom of Darkness in Jesus Name!

Matthew 18:18-20 NKJV
18 "Assuredly, I say to you, whatever you bind on earth will be bound in heaven, and whatever you loose on earth will be loosed in heaven.
19 "Again I say to you that if two of you agree on earth concerning anything that they ask, it will be done for them by My Father in heaven.
20 For where two or three are gathered together in My name, I am there in the midst of them."

I was listening to an Evangelist who is a former Satanic High Priest on TBN some time ago and he shed some light on the Satan's kingdom. He said that the Kingdom of Darkness is not divided. They are completely unified to bring division to the Kingdom of God and the people of God. I know this doesn't appear to make sense, but as I stated before, the dividers are united to divide us.

One of the most important spiritual weapons that we have is the power of agreement. One reason the enemy fights us so much and tries to keep us from coming into agreement, is that he knows how powerful we can be when we come together in prayer, agreement and unity.

He knows that the power of God moves mightily when we are on one accord, and that God does his best work when the saints are of one mind and one spirit. Listen to the Word!

"Again I say to you that if two of you agree on earth concerning anything that they ask, it will be done for them by My Father in heaven. For where two or three are gathered together in My name, I am there in the midst of them."
Matthew 18:19-20 NKJV

Even in the Old Testament we find that the spirit of agreement was powerful in Gen 11: 1-9.

Unity in Building the Tower of Babel

Genesis 11:1-9 NKJV
1 Now the whole earth had one language and one speech.
2 And it came to pass, as they journeyed from the east, that they found a plain in the land of Shinar, and they dwelt there.
3 Then they said to one another, "Come, let us make bricks and bake them thoroughly." They had brick for stone, and they had asphalt for mortar.
4 And they said, "Come, let us build ourselves a city, and a tower whose top is in the heavens; let us make a name for ourselves, lest we be scattered abroad over the face of the whole earth."

5 But the LORD came down to see the city and the tower which the sons of men had built.

6 And the LORD said, "Indeed the people are one and they all have one language, and this is what they begin to do; now nothing that they propose to do will be withheld from them.

7 Come, let Us go down and there confuse their language, that they may not understand one another's speech."

8 So the LORD scattered them abroad from there over the face of all the earth, and they ceased building the city.

9 Therefore its name is called Babel, because there the LORD confused the language of all the earth; and from there the LORD scattered them abroad over the face of all the earth.

Do you see what was at work here? The people were as one and they were attempting to build a tower to the heavens. The Bible says that they wanted to make a name for themselves. I want you to get a picture of this.

They were trying to build a city and tower to heaven to make a name for themselves. In other words because of their egos they wanted to go as high as they could, to reach heaven and God. This is nothing but pride.

The spirit of pride always seeks to go higher than everyone else. The spirit of pride always wants to make a name for itself! Here is the revelation in these passages of scripture. The Bible says in Genesis 11: 5, the LORD came down to see the city and tower which the sons of men had built. Now get this revelation. In verse 6, the LORD said, **"Indeed the people are one and they all have one language, and this is what they begin to do; now nothing that they propose to do will be withheld from them.**

Did you hear that? Although they were trying to do something totally against the will of God, they were as one in making progress in building this tower. The LORD then said in verse 7, "I have to go down and confuse their language because if they accomplish this, there is nothing that they will not be able to accomplish. Why? Because they are in agreement and they are as one!

There is also another example in the Old Testament that is profound. Let's take a look!

2 Chronicles 5:12-14 NKJV
12 and the Levites who were the singers, all those of Asaph and Heman and Jeduthun, with their sons and their brethren, stood at the east end of the altar, clothed in white linen, having cymbals, stringed instruments and harps, and with them one hundred and twenty priests sounding with trumpets--
13 indeed it came to pass, when the trumpeters and singers were as one, to make one sound to be heard in praising and

thanking the LORD, and when they lifted up their voice with the trumpets and cymbals and instruments of music, and praised the LORD, saying: "For He is good, For His mercy endures forever," that the house, the house of the LORD, was filled with a cloud,
14 so that the priests could not continue ministering because of the cloud; for the glory of the LORD filled the house of God.

Did you get that? When the trumpeters and singers were as one to make one sound they were in agreement. There was no one who was a big "I" and there was no one who was a little "u." They were as "One" praising and lifting their voices to the LORD and the glory of the LORD filled the house! Isn't this amazing! The people of God were in agreement and the glory of the LORD fell afresh upon them! I believe that the very essence of God is unity. He moves in the midst of unity and does his best work when we are unified.

Peters Revelation and Agreement With God

Matthew 16:13-19 NKJV
13 When Jesus came into the region of Caesarea Philippi, He asked His disciples, saying, "Who do men say that I, the Son of Man am?"
14 So they said, "Some say John the Baptist, some Elijah, and others Jeremiah or one of the prophets."
15 He said to them, "But who do you say that I am?"

16 Simon Peter answered and said, "You are the Christ, the Son of the living God."

We must remember that in order to receive power from on high, we must come into agreement with the revealed Word of God and Holy Spirit revelation concerning Jesus Christ. When Peter acknowledged who Christ was – He came into agreement with the Holy Spirit inspired revelation from the Father that Jesus was the Christ, the Messiah, The Son of the living God.

If you are not in agreement with God's Word. How can you get the understanding and revelation that God desires to release to you? In other words, how can you have power if you are not in agreement with the Word?

When you acknowledge who Christ is, and recognize that he has all power in his hand, you come into agreement with his Word. And we find that when you come into agreement with his Word. God commands a blessing. Look at Matt 16: 17-19:

17 Jesus answered and said to him, "Blessed are you, Simon Bar-Jonah, for flesh and blood has not revealed this to you, but My Father who is in heaven. 18 And I also say to you that you are Peter, and on this rock I will build My church, and the gates of Hades shall not prevail against it.
19 And I will give you the keys of the kingdom of heaven, and whatever you bind on earth will be

bound in heaven, and whatever you loose on earth will be loosed in heaven."

The Apostle Paul and Agreement

The Apostle Paul said something profound in Rom 15: 5-7 concerning agreement.

Romans 15:5-7 NKJV
**5 Now may the God of patience and comfort grant you to be like-minded toward one another, according to Christ Jesus,
6 that you may with one mind and one mouth glorify the God and Father of our Lord Jesus Christ.**
7 Therefore receive one another, just as Christ also received us, to the glory of God.

Isn't this a profound scripture? Paul is praying that the Saints be like minded toward one another, and that they be of one mind and one mouth glorify God! In others words they would unify as one and be in agreement with one another.

The following are nine points of wisdom concerning unity, oneness and agreement:

1. God is all about unity and relationships!
2. God has created everything to have an order.
3. Unity and love are divine attributes of God.
4. Anything or any person that does not submit to the

divine order of God is out of order.

5. God never meant for there to be cliques or groups in the Body of Christ.

6. Although there are cell groups and study groups, they all belong to one body.

7. The reason why we can't move forward many times is because of two things:

  a. There are entities within that hinder the spirit of unity.

  b. There are entities outside that want to destroy us.

8. The reason why many local churches can't move forward is because of disagreement and unity problems.

Here are some questions to ponder and consider?

1. Where does the LORD command the blessing?
2. Why should we unify?
3. What can we do to unify more?

CHAPTER 6

Division is a Work of the Flesh

"Lest Satan should take advantage of us, for we are not ignorant of his devices."
2 Corinthians 2:11 NKJV

The Apostle Paul said that if we are ignorant of Satan's device he will take advantage of us. This means that we have to be wise and not allow the enemy to deceive and destroy us with his devices. Six devices that he uses against the Church and the people of God are: disunity, division, dissention, disunion, discord, and disagreement. Of course these are not the only devices but these are the most common devices that he uses against families, churches, leaders, marriages, and friendships.

People of God, I want you to know that division is a work of the flesh and anyone that entertains it is operating in the flesh. Unity is a spiritual and heavenly principle throughout the Bible. In 1 Cor 1: 10-11, the Apostle Paul gives us some wisdom on division in the church. Let's read!

1 Corinthians 1:10-13 NKJV
10 Now I plead with you, brethren, by the name of our Lord Jesus Christ, **that you all speak the same thing, and that there be no divisions among you,** but that you be perfectly joined together in the same mind and in the same judgment. 11 For it has been declared to me concerning you, my brethren, by those of Chloe's household, that there are contentions among you.

12 Now I say this, that each of you says, "I am of Paul or I am of Apollos," or "I am of Cephas or "I am of Christ."
13 Is Christ divided? Was Paul crucified for you? Or were you baptized in the name of Paul?

Isn't this an interesting text in the Bible? When we read this we find that Paul is admonishing and rebuking the Corinthian church for their divisions and possibly cliques in the church. In verse 10, Paul is pleading with them in the name of the LORD to speak the same thing and that there be no divisions among the people of God.
In other words, do not disagree, but unify and agree. He goes on to plead with them to be perfectly joined together in the same mind, and in the same judgment.

Why is this important? Because Paul understands that the primary device of the enemy is division, and that the people of God must be perfectly joined together with the same mind and judgment as it relates to the church and spiritual things.

Paul goes on to add in verses 11-13,
11 For it has been declared to me concerning you, my brethren, by those of Chloe's household, that there are contentions among you.
12 Now I say this that each of you says, "I am of Paul, or I am of Apollos," or "I am of Cephas," or "I am of Christ."
13 Is Christ divided? Was Paul crucified for you? Or were you baptized in the name of Paul?

I love these verses because we need more people like Chloe who will let the leadership know what is going on! Obviously, there were some spirit led people that saw what was going on and reported it to Paul. This is exactly what we need in the Body of Christ!

People of God, the Holy Spirit has showed me that there are indeed divisions in the Body of Christ that need to be addressed. God has truly blessed us as a body of believers, but I believe that we have not scratched the surface as it relates to doing the will of God! Why? Because of divisions in the Body of Christ! Chloe and her household reported to Paul that there were contentions among the people of God, and the division was getting out of order affecting the church and the people of God.

In Verse 12, Paul addresses the division. People were beginning to get into cliques and groups by saying I am of Paul, I am of Apollo's, I am of Cephas, or I am of Christ! Can you see what is going on here? People were starting to get unfocused on Kingdom business and began to lift up personalities. Let me digress for a moment.

Isn't this the state of the Body of Christ today? We find this spirit at work many times were people follow after personalities or certain churches and they say, "I am of this preacher, or I am of this church, or my Pastor is so and so, or I go to this church. As if that person or church can save your soul! Paul hits the nail right on the head and addresses the issue in verse 13.

13 Is Christ divided? Was Paul crucified for you? Or were you baptized in the name of Paul?

In other words, this is isn't about any one individual.

71

This is about Jesus Christ, LORD of Lords and King of Kings. Paul said, "Was I crucified for you?" or "Were you baptized in the name of Paul for the remission of your sins?" Paul is saying, this is not about personalities or churches. It is about Jesus Christ, who is the Good Shepherd, Chief Shepherd, and Great Shepherd. (John 10: 11, Heb 13: 20, 1 Peter 5: 4)

This is why I love the Bible! Regardless of what unbelievers say, everything that pertains to life and godliness for the church is in the Bible. God addresses everything that we need to succeed as a church, but many times we ignore it.

We even see this spirit at work in denominations, organizations and groups. For example, if you are not of this group, or if you don't praise, worship or even prophesy like a particular group, they may say that it is not of God.

Brothers and Sisters, division is a work of the flesh and we have lost our way if we allow this spirit from hell to permeate our churches and congregations. The Bible says there is one Lord, one faith and one baptism. (Eph 4: 5) Although there are local communities of Christ, there is one ecclesia which is the true church of Jesus Christ.

Regardless of our denomination or organization, we all have something to add to the ecclesia of God. When I think about it, I have been exposed to various denominations and non-denominations since I was a child.

I was raised in the Baptist church and attended a

Methodist church in my teen years. After I joined the military in 1993, I got filled with the Holy Spirit in the Pentecostal church, learned how to live holy in the Holiness church and got empowered in the Apostolic church! Some of you may laugh but this was the journey of my faith in Christ! Wow, what a journey!

Nevertheless, I learned something from all those churches in my walk of faith in Christ, and one thing I can truly say. I have met some wonderful Saints and leaders in many of those denominational and non-denominational churches that impacted my life even to this day!

Racism and Division in the Church

Let's also address the issue of racism in the church, because we do know for a fact that division is a byproduct of racism in the church as well. There are some people who consider themselves to be ministers of Christ but embrace racism. This too is a work of the flesh. There is no way that you can be called a servant of God and embrace racism in any form or fashion.

Racism can be practiced from any race of people that claim to be above another group of people. I totally denounce racism in any form or fashion but embrace the truth of God's Word. When you read the book of Revelation we find the following:

Revelation 7:9 KJV
9 After this I beheld, and, lo, a great multitude, which no man could number, of all nations, and

kindred's, and people, and tongues, stood before the throne, and before the Lamb, clothed with white robes, and palms in their hands.

Did you read what the scripture said? There was a great multitude of people that no man could number. It consisted of people of all nations, kindred's, and tongues that stood before the throne of God. I believe that is the Body of Christ and those that chose to serve, love and obey the Word of God. It was a number that no man could number, but they all loved God and stood before the throne of the One True God.

There are demonic entities today that are trying to turn back the hands of time so that people of color can be subjugated to racism and Jim Crow laws again. This too is a divisive lie from the pit of hell. The true church of Jesus Christ is not divided by racism. We do know that in the times of slavery there were people who used the Bible to keep people under the yoke of bondage in slavery. But the times have changed and there is an awakening among God's people who see through all the devices of the devil. They know that the devil is working overtime to sow a seed of division through racism to divide the church and ultimately the country.

A true servant of the LORD will speak out against it and not embrace it. It does not matter whether you live in the north, south, east or west, suburban or rural area. It does not matter if your church is in America, Europe, Asia or Africa, Jesus has one true church, and God's church is not racist.

If your church is racist against people of any color,

and your Pastor is racist, they have missed the mark and need deliverance. There are people of all races who have the love of God in their hearts. There are also people who are racist, bigoted and need hands layed on them so they can repent and come to their senses in Jesus Name!

Division is indeed a Work of the Flesh

In the book of Galatians chapter 5, the Apostle Paul addresses division again. This time he is making his point that division is no different than any other sin which is a work of the flesh, and is not of the Kingdom of God. Let's read! I have used the NKJV for clarity:

Galatians 5:16-25 NKJV
16 I say then: Walk in the Spirit, and you shall not fulfill the lust of the flesh.
17 For the flesh lusts against the Spirit, and the Spirit against the flesh; and these are contrary to one another, so that you do not do the things that you wish.
18 But if you are led by the Spirit, you are not under the law.
19 Now the works of the flesh are evident, which are: adultery, fornication, uncleanness, lewdness,
20 idolatry, sorcery, hatred, contentions, jealousies, outbursts of wrath, selfish ambitions, **dissensions,** heresies,
21 envy, murders, drunkenness, revelries, and the like; of which I tell you beforehand, just as I also told you in time past, that those who practice such things will not inherit the kingdom of God.
22 But the fruit of the Spirit is love, joy, peace, longsuffering, kindness, goodness, faithfulness,

23 gentleness, self-control. Against such there is no law.
24 And those who are Christ's have crucified the flesh with its passions and desires.

Paul said that the fruit of the flesh is evident in verse 19-21. Dissension can be defined as disagreement that leads to discord. Synonyms or words that are the same as dissension are disagreement, discord, disunion and even strife. These are the devices of Satan and they are used against the church to keep the people of God divided.

This is why we need to walk in the spirit and live by the spirit. Spirit led people know the difference between flesh and spirit. Dissension is listed among all the other sins to include idolatry, jealousies, murder, adultery, fornication and much more.

As we can see, division is truly a work of the flesh. It is my prayer that each and every person who understands the importance of unity in the Body of Christ will begin to pray and unify with other spirit led churches, so that we can destroy the works of the wicked one, and bring God glory in Jesus name!

Chapter 7

One Vision and One Spirit

John 17:20-23 NKJV
20 "I do not pray for these alone, but also for those
who will believe in Me through their word;
21 that they all may be one, as You, Father, are in Me,
and I in You; that they also may be one in Us, that the
world may believe that You sent Me.
22 And the glory which You gave Me I have given
them, that they may be one just as We are one:
23 I in them, and You in Me; that they may be made
perfect in one, and that the world may know that You
have sent Me, and have loved them as You have loved
Me.

One of the most powerful prayers ever prayed in
the Bible is in John chapter 17. The reason why this
prayer is so powerful is because it was prayed by our
LORD Jesus Christ, and contains some profound
wisdom on oneness and unity.

I believe Christ prayed this prayer because he
understood that in order to accomplish the Kingdom
agenda of God, the people would have to be unified
with one spirit and one vision. How many of us know
that there is one Kingdom agenda as it relates to the
preaching and teaching of the Gospel? There may be
many ministries and operations of those ministries
but there is one Gospel.

Since there is one Lord, one faith and one baptism,
that means that the people of God and the churches
of God must have one spirit and one vision. When

God gives a church or ministry a vision, there can only be one vision.

All churches and ministries should have a vision. Whenever you join a church, that church should have a God given vision in place. Of course that vision should line up with the overall mission and vision of God's Kingdom agenda. Why? because there is nothing worse than the blind leading the blind, which is not good, because they will both fall into a pit. (Matt 15: 14)

Before Jesus left the earth, he gave us a mission and a vision in Matthew 28: 19-20:

19 Go therefore and make disciples of all the nations, baptizing them in the name of the Father and of the Son and of the Holy Spirit,
20 teaching them to observe all things that I have commanded you.

Anytime God gives us something great the devil always tries to emulate what God creates. God is a creator, Satan is an imitator. God gives us a vision, but Satan brings division.

Division is when there are two visions or two separate visions. Division is a divided vision which means two or more people are not in agreement. There can only be one vision.

When there are two visions there are two mindsets, two thought patterns, and two different ideas on how to accomplish a goal. This cannot be! There can be many ideas as we brainstorm in relation to fulfilling the vision, but there can only be one vision. If there are two visions, this can lead to division, and Jesus said the following about division.

Luke 11:17 KJV
17 But he, knowing their thoughts, said unto them, Every kingdom divided against itself is brought to desolation; and a house divided against a house falls.

Vision is an interesting word. This is also where we get the word Super-vision. When you have a vision or idea on your job you probably have to go through a Supervisor who has supervision over you and others.

It's interesting because if you come up with an idea or have a vision on your job, most likely it has to go to someone who has "super-vision over you."

A very important factor for every person to remember in the body of Christ is that the staff, leaders, and members must have the same spirit and anointing that the Visionary has as it relates to the vision.

It's important that all God ordained support ministry connected to the vision have the same spirit of the Visionary. This is why when people leave an organization it's normally because they no longer support the vision of that organization.

"Can two walk together, except they be agreed?" Amos 3:3 KJV

How many of us know that it is important to keep the spirit of unity at all costs because we are not ignorant of Satan's devices.

It's important that every member that is connected to a church or ministry, especially the leadership connect with the vision and support the vision. God will appoint and anoint those he has called to connect to the vision of the house, and will put the same spirit on them that is on the visionary. This is so important because I have found in many years of ministry that we can accomplish so much more when we have one vision, one mind and one spirit.

In the book Numbers chapter 11, the LORD did something interesting with Moses and seventy Elders. Let's read:

Numbers 11:16-17 NKJV
16 So the LORD said to Moses: "Gather to Me seventy men of the elders of Israel, whom you know to be the elders of the people and officers over them; bring them to the tabernacle of meeting, that they may stand there with you.
17 Then I will come down and talk with you there. I will take of the Spirit that is upon you and will put the same upon them; and they shall bear the burden of the people with you, that you may not bear it yourself alone.

The Lord never intended that the visionary bear the burden of the vision alone. The Vision is not for the visionary alone, it is for the people of God, the body of Christ, and the community. It is to save souls, and to bring people to purpose in Christ Jesus!

So Moses did what God instructed and look what happened:

Numbers 11:24-25 NKJV
24 So Moses went out and told the people the words

of the LORD, and he gathered the seventy men of the elders of the people and placed them around the tabernacle.

25 Then the LORD came down in the cloud, and spoke to him, and took of the Spirit that was upon him, and placed the same upon the seventy elders; and it happened, when the Spirit rested upon them, that they prophesied, although they never did so again.

Here we see that all of Moses support ministry who were the Elders or leaders were given the same spirit and anointing that was on him. God took of the spirit that was on the Shepherd or visionary to anoint all seventy of his support staff elders.

It is interesting that the Lord took of the spirit that was on Moses and placed it on them. Notice the LORD did not say, "I will take of my Spirit," but it was the Spirit that was upon Moses. Does anyone have the spirit of the visionary?

It is extremely important that the people in a local church catch the visionary's spirit and vision. In fact Proverbs 29: 18 says, "Where there is no vision the people perish or cease to live."

In order for life and prosperity to flow in people's lives, they must be connected and or faithful to the vision that God has ordained for the ministry that they are connected too.

God orders our footsteps to a particular ministry some for a season, some for a reason, and when they submit to the vision and have the same spirit as the visionary; the Lord releases a supernatural anointing and grace to fulfill purpose.

It's interesting that in Numbers chapter 13 the LORD told Moses to send 12 men leaders of every tribe to spy out the land that he was giving to them! Did you get that? God told them to check out the land that he already had purposed for them, and was giving to them. But only two of them came back with a good report.

"And the LORD spoke to Moses, saying, "Send men to spy out the land of Canaan, which I am giving to the children of Israel; from each tribe of their fathers you shall send a man, everyone a leader among them."
Numbers 13:1-2 NKJV

When you read the story, we find that God told them to spy and check out the land. Instead of agreeing with God's vision for them and receiving by faith what God had already purposed for them, they saw something else. In other words, they had a "different vision."

The Lord wanted them to receive by faith what he had already predestined, purposed, prophesied and promised for them, but they saw something else. Could it be that the reason the church has not experienced unprecedented power and anointing is because we all see something different?

When we receive by faith and agree with God's Word and the vision he has for us, the result is life more abundantly! There were two men who believed the report of the LORD and they were Joshua and Caleb.

The Bible says that they had a different spirit. In other words they believed God and were ready to fulfill the vision of God to take possession of the Promised Land.

"But My servant Caleb, because he has a different spirit in him and has followed Me fully, I will bring into the land where he went, and his descendants shall inherit it."
Numbers 14:24 NKJV

"Except for Caleb the son of Jephunneh and Joshua the son of Nun, you shall by no means enter the land which I swore I would make you dwell in."
Numbers 14:30 NKJV

They had the same spirit that Moses had and believed the Word of the LORD. Can you imagine that ten out of twelve men did not enter in because of unbelief?

God's vision for the Children of Israel was to spy out the land, then take possession of the land. But they had a different spirit and a different vision. They said, "We cannot take possession of the land."

Numbers 13:31-33 NKJV
31 But the men who had gone up with him said, "We are not able to go up against the people, for they are stronger than we."
32 And they gave the children of Israel a bad report of the land which they had spied out, saying, "The land through which we have gone as spies is a land that devours its inhabitants, and all the people whom we saw in it are men of great stature.

33 There we saw the giants (the descendants of Anak came from the giants); and we were like grasshoppers in our own sight, and so we were in their sight."

Just as it was then, that same spirit is in the Body of Christ now. There are people who always think they have greater wisdom than God, and even the leaders whom they are connected to. This is the reason people wander from church to church without being committed or linked to God given vision.

So many people fail to realize that God gives leaders a vision to lead his people into their promised land of purpose and inheritance. Yet there are many of God's people who will never receive their promised inheritance because they never connect to the vision, therefore they perish rather than prosper.

"For the lips of a priest should keep knowledge, and people should seek the law from his mouth; For he is the messenger of the LORD of hosts.
Malachi 2:7 NKJV

God gives and uses leaders to speak to his people and to lead his people. Yet many times people do not receive from that leader. It is so imperative that every person connect to a church and leader where they can receive and grow in the grace of God. This is why you should pray to the LORD and speak to the leadership before joining a church.

Don't join a church because they have good music, good preaching, and a bunch of ministries. You should join a church because they have a great vision! Don't get me wrong, music, preaching and ministries for the family are important, but ensure they have a great vision as well.

No wonder the Apostle Paul was so direct in speaking to the church at Corinth about unity, divisions, and contentions. When there is one vision, one spirit, and one focused objective among the people, God moves supernaturally on behalf of his visionary and the vision.

When God begins to move supernaturally for the visionary, the people that support him wholeheartedly will be supernaturally empowered and will prosper as well. When there is unity and oneness in intent, purpose and plan, it allows the supernatural power of the Holy Spirit to move on behalf of the people and the vision.

I want to tell you a parable that I once read about the important of unity.

There is an old legend about a herd of mules that was attacked nightly by a pack of wolves from a nearby forest. When the wolves came, the mules began kicking viciously in all directions. Consequently the mules maimed and injured each other while the agile wolves escaped unharmed.

Finally, a wise old mule called the rest of the mules together for a conference because he had a vision and a plan to defeat the wolves. That night the wolves came snarling and yelping from the forest as usual, but instead of the mules kicking in all directions, they all ran and put their heads together in a circle and began kicking outward, injuring and hurting many of the wolves.

The wolves were put to flight, and the mules did no harm to each other. The moral of the story is that Christians need to get their heads together and kick outward against the forces of iniquity.

Let's stop kicking at each other, and hurting each other. The world must sometimes wonder if the Body of Christ has any heads to put together, because we are always kicking and hurting one another instead of the enemy. Selah.

Brothers and Sisters in Christ, it's time to put our heads together as one so that we can accomplish the God given vision given to us. The visionary can't do it alone. Everyone must ask the Lord what is my purpose here for the vision. What have you called me to do in this church ministry while I am here?

There are many people that join churches today but never connect to the vision of the house. Some people only show up when they are in need. When was the last time you asked your Pastor, the visionary what can you do to help bring the vision to pass? Every growing church requires members of the body to contribute with their time, talents and treasure in order to do Kingdom ministry for Jesus Christ.

Chapter 8

The Power of Oneness in Jesus Christ

As we endeavor to do the will of the LORD, there is a one very important thing that we must be mindful of in our walk with Christ Jesus. We must all be on one accord with one another. This is how we defeat the forces of darkness.

One of the oldest tactics of the enemy has been to "divide and conquer." This is the reason why churches split, marriages fell, friendships break up, and family members are at odds with one another. Remember what Ephesians 6: 12 says:

"For we wrestle not against flesh and blood, but against principalities, against powers, against the rulers of the darkness of this world, against spiritual wickedness in high places."
Ephesians 6:12 KJV

Remember Paul said that our wrestle is not against flesh and blood, but against the spiritual forces of darkness that cause division and destruction. This is why we must release what offenses we have against one another, and get in unity.

Have you ever seen a military formation where they are marching together? Everyone is in lockstep, in harmony and on one accord! You can sense the power of unity amongst them.

I can remember when I joined the military many years ago and went to boot camp in San Diego, California. When I reported to boot camp, I looked at all the guys that were there and we were a motley crew. I mean we were some of the most messed up people I have ever seen, at least I thought so. I said to myself, wow, what in the world have I gotten myself in! We all looked a hot mess!

There were black, white, Hispanic, and Asian recruits that were joining the Navy who came from all over the United States to join the Navy and serve our country.

What is amazing is after eight weeks of training, physical fitness, and Navy training we were all on one accord, marching together and singing cadences. We were a team, a company and we were in perfectly unified! It was truly a proud moment when we graduated, because we had been molded into a company of one!

Even in sports when everybody knows their positions and assignments, victory is also certain against a team that is divided or confused. Someone even said that when geese are flying south they fly in unity in a "V" formation.

Listen to this: Many years ago a team of scientists conducted a study about the benefits of unity. They taped heart monitors to a group of pelicans that were trained to fly behind a small airplane. They discovered that the heart rates of the birds were lower when flying together in a "V" formation rather than flying solo.

According to scientist, migrating birds use the "squadron" formation because it allows them to glide more often, conserving energy. The aerodynamic "V" shape reduces the air resistance, allowing the geese to cover longer distances. In fact, a flock of geese can fly 70 percent farther by adopting the "V" shape rather than flying in isolation.

The "V" formation may offer other benefits as well. Each bird has an unobstructed field of vision, allowing flock members to see each other and communicate while in flight. The goose at the head of the V is not necessarily the leader of the flock. Apparently, geese take turns leading. As one bird tires, it drops to the back of the formation and another takes its place. Isn't this amazing! Now that's what I call teamwork!

Even in the Church, Pastors can't run ministries and churches alone. It takes a team of faithful, committed, loyal saints who understand unity to do great Kingdom ministry.

Now, let's talk about the power of ONE. In the Bible there is a prayer that is called the "Shema." Many Jews, Messianic Jews, and Hebrews still recite this prayer.
It is used as a centerpiece of all their morning and evening prayers. It is considered one of the most important prayers. Let's break the prayer down. Here is the prayer:

"Shema Yisrael Adonai Eloheinu Echad"

Shema (A three part word) — listen, or hear and "act on"
Yisrael — Israel, in the sense of the people or the congregation of Israel
Adonai — translated as "Lord"

Eloheinu — our God, the word "El" or "Elohei" signifying God. We know it as Elohim.
Echad — the Hebrew word for number "1"

This is translated as "Hear, O Israel! The LORD our God, the LORD is one!"

This prayer comes to us from Deuteronomy chapter 6: 4-5.

Deuteronomy 6:4-7 NKJV
4 "Hear, O Israel: The LORD our God, the LORD is one!
5 You shall love the LORD your God with all your heart, with all your soul, and with all your strength.

As a matter of fact in the book *Biblical Mathematics: Keys to Scripture Numerics* by Evangelist Ed Vallowe, ONE is the number in the Bible that stands for UNITY. Unity is an important doctrine. It symbolizes the unity of God. It stands for that which is unique and alone.

The Apostle John echoed this important fact in 1 John 5: 7 when he said: For there are three that bear witness in heaven: the Father, the Word, and the Holy Spirit; and these three are ONE.

Who was he talking about when he said the WORD? He was referring to Jesus the Christ, The Messiah, the Son of the Living God. We know it as the Holy Trinity which is the Father, Son and Holy Spirit.

A Muslim once told me he didn't understand this because we are referring to three Gods. I said no my friend, your math is incorrect. It is not 1 + 1 + 1 because that would equal 3. It is 1 x 1 x 1 which equals 1.

How many of us know that we serve One God? As a Christian we don't believe in many ways to God. We believe in one God. Don't ever let anyone try to change your mind. I tell them to read what Jesus said in the scriptures:

"Then the Jews surrounded Him and said to Him, "How long do You keep us in doubt? If You are the Christ, tell us plainly." Jesus answered them, "I told you, and you do not believe. **The works that I do in My Father's name, they bear witness of Me.**"
John 10:24-25 NKJV

"I and My Father are one."
John 10:30 NKJV

"That they all may be one, as You, Father, are in Me, and I in You; that they also may be one in us, that the world may believe that You sent Me."
John 17:21 NKJV

So we see here that Jesus emphasized the importance of unity among the believers because division is a work of the enemy and of the flesh. Let's review what the scriptures say about division.

"But Jesus knew their thoughts, and said to them: "Every kingdom **divided** against itself is brought to desolation, and every city or house divided against itself will not stand."
Matthew 12:25 NKJV

"Now I plead with you, brethren, by the name of our Lord Jesus Christ, that you all speak the same thing, and that there be no **divisions** among you, but that you be perfectly joined together in the same mind and in the same judgment."
1 Corinthians 1:10 NKJV

"For you are still carnal. For where there are envy, strife, and **divisions among you**, are you not carnal and behaving like mere men?"
1 Corinthians 3:3 NKJV

"Now the works of the flesh are evident, which are: adultery, fornication, uncleanness, lewdness, idolatry, sorcery, hatred, contentions, jealousies, outbursts of wrath, selfish ambitions, **dissensions**, and heresies."
Galatians 5:19-20 NKJV

Now let's contrast some scriptures as it relates to unity:

2 Chronicles 5:13-14 NKJV
13 indeed it came to pass, **when the trumpeters and singers were as one, to make one sound to be heard in praising and thanking the LORD,** and when they lifted up their voice with the trumpets and cymbals and instruments of music, and praised the LORD, saying: "For He is good, For His mercy endures forever," that the house, the house of the LORD, was filled with a cloud,
14 so that the priests could not continue ministering because of the cloud; for the glory of the LORD filled the house of God.

2 Chronicles 20:1-4 NKJV
1 It happened after this that the people of Moab with the people of Ammon, and others with them besides the Ammonites, came to battle against Jehoshaphat.
2 Then some came and told Jehoshaphat, saying, "A great multitude is coming against you from beyond the sea, from Syria; and they are in Hazazon Tamar" (which is En Gedi).
3 And Jehoshaphat feared, and set himself to seek the LORD, and proclaimed a fast throughout all Judah.
4 So Judah gathered together to ask help from the LORD; and from all the cities of Judah they came to seek the LORD.

Acts 2:1-4 NKJV
1 When the Day of Pentecost had fully come, they were all with one accord in one place.
2 And suddenly there came a sound from heaven, as of a rushing mighty wind, and it filled the whole house where they were sitting.
3 Then there appeared to them divided tongues, as of fire, and one sat upon each of them.
4 And they were all filled with the Holy Spirit and began to speak with other tongues, as the Spirit gave them utterance.

Acts 2:44-47 NKJV
44 Now all who believed were together, and had all things in common,
45 and sold their possessions and goods, and divided them among all, as anyone had need.
46 So continuing daily with one accord in the temple, and breaking bread from house to house, they ate their food with gladness and

simplicity of heart,
47 praising God and having favor with all the people.
And the Lord added to the church daily those who
were being saved.

Ephesians 4:1-6 NKJV
1 I, therefore, the prisoner of the Lord, beseech you to
walk worthy of the calling with which you were
called,
2 with all lowliness and gentleness, with
longsuffering, bearing with one another in love,
**3 endeavoring to keep the unity of the Spirit
in the bond of peace.
4 There is one body and one Spirit, just as you
were called in one hope of your calling;
5 one Lord, one faith, one baptism;
6 one God and Father of all, who is above all,
and through all, and in you all.**

One of the sad things about the church is that we
have gotten comfortable in division. There is a story
that is told about the horrors of slavery. The slave
owners would put the light skinned Negroes against
the black skinned Negroes to create a division and
dislike for each other to strengthen the bondage of
slavery, creating a division among the people. How
many of us know there is nothing new under the sun?

This is the device and tactic of the devil. He is still
doing the same thing today! Create a wedge or
division in the body that will divide us. If there is any
group of people that should understand the power of
the unity it should be the church of our LORD Jesus
Christ!

The Church must come to the full understanding of who we are in Christ. We should be of one mind and one spirit. If we disagree, we should be able to talk about it and put some Word on it! We may disagree, but I guarantee that the Bible will bring us to agreement!

If you disagree with a leader, brother or sister in the church, don't go gossip and put it all over social media and add fuel to the fire. You should reason together according to scripture and put the devil under your feet.

Mature believers understand that this is the Biblical way to resolve disagreements in the church. Now believe me, I do understand that there are some people who you may not be able to resolve issues. The main thing to do is owe no man anything but love according to the scriptures, and to follow the ways of peace.

"Owe no one anything except to love one another, for he who loves another has fulfilled the law."
Romans 13:8 NKJV

"Follow peace with all men, and holiness, without which no man shall see the Lord."
Hebrews 12:14 KJV

I am reminded of a story in the book of Genesis where Abraham and Lot had a disagreement. Listen to the way Abraham the man of God resolved the issue. Let's read!

Genesis 13:5-9 NKJV
5 Lot also, who went with Abram, had flocks and

herds and tents.

6 Now the land was not able to support them, that they might dwell together, for their possessions were so great that they could not dwell together.

7 And there was strife between the herdsmen of Abram's livestock and the herdsmen of Lot's livestock. The Canaanites and the Perizzites then dwelt in the land.

8 So Abram said to Lot, "Please let there be no strife between you and me, and between my herdsmen and your herdsmen; for we are brethren.

9 Is not the whole land before you? Please separate from me. If you take the left, then I will go to the right; or, if you go to the right, then I will go to the left."

Many of us know the story. There was strife between the camps of Abraham and Lot because they had so much substance between the two of them. Abraham took the high road and said in verse 8, "Brother, "Please let there be no strife between you and me, and between my herdsmen and your herdsmen; for we are brethren."

Did you get that? Let there be no strife between you and me, for we are brothers! He goes on to add in verse 9, is not the whole land before you? Please separate from me.
If you take the left, then I will go to the right; or, if you go to the right, then I will go to the left."

Abraham basically said, "Brother, instead of us being in strife, upset, angry and bitter, let's just separate! You go to the left, and I will go to the right, or you go to the left and I will go to the right.

Wow, can you see the wisdom and maturity of Abraham? Abraham basically said, "Lot you are not going to mess up my blessing with the LORD, so let's just do the right thing and keep the peace by separating! We find later in Genesis 13 that Lot chose Sodom and do I need to say more? We know the end of that story!

What is interesting is that after Lot separated from Abraham, the LORD pronounces a wonderful prophetic blessing upon him!

Genesis 13:14-18 NKJV
14 **And the LORD said to Abram, after Lot had separated from him:** "Lift your eyes now and look from the place where you are--northward, southward, eastward, and westward;
15 for all the land which you see I give to you and your descendants forever.
16 And I will make your descendants as the dust of the earth; so that if a man could number the dust of the earth, then your descendants also could be numbered.
17 Arise, walk in the land through its length and its width, for I give it to you."
18 Then Abram moved his tent, and went and dwelt by the terebinth trees of Mamre, which are in Hebron, and built an altar there to the LORD.

Now, I hate to say this, but sometimes you have to just let some people go that are not in agreement with you. The worst thing you need is someone tagging along that is hindering your purpose and destiny in Christ. What is amazing is that after Lot leaves, God spoke!

I want to encourage someone who is reading this. You may have had someone depart from you for whatever reason. It may be a friend, a member of the church, or even someone you were close to. Regardless of whatever reason it is, let them go. As a Pastor I have learned the secret of contentment as Paul said in Phil 4: 11:

"Not that I speak in regard to need, for I have learned in whatever state I am, to be content."
Philippians 4:11 NKJV

I would rather have 5 people who agree with me, than 50 who disagree with me. 5 people in agreement can do more than 50 in disagreement! I have been Pastoring for many years and I have seen people come and go. There were some I hated to see go, and others, I was glad to see them go.

Why? Because we all need to move on with our destiny in Christ without hindrance. Is this not the mindset of Abraham? He knew that division would be counterproductive to his purpose and destiny and said Lot, let's just do the right thing and separate!

In order to keep the spirit of unity we must not be ignorant of Satan's devices. Many times what happens is that someone will get offended or get mad about something. Then they begin to tell half-truths which spread like a flu virus. Division can be birthed out of the spirit of offense, and the spirit of offense will open the door to discord and even dissension.

The book of Proverbs gives us some good wisdom about offenses and divisions:

"A brother offended is harder to win than a strong city, And contentions are like the bars of a castle." Proverbs 18:19 NKJV

We should always endeavor to keep the spirit of unity in the bond of peace. Many times this does not happen, but we must follow scripture to get the victory. The greatest way to get the victory is by walking in the spirit. Because when we walk in the spirit we will do all things in love.

"And above all things have fervent love for one another, for "Love will cover a multitude of sins." 1 Peter 4:8 NKJV

"A new commandment I give to you, that you love one another; as I have loved you, that you also love one another. By this all will know that you are My disciples, if you have love for one another." John 13:34-35 NKJV

Remember according to scripture, love and unity are two solid strong principles that enable us to accomplish all that God has put in our hearts. I believe that there are no greater principles than love and unity.

I believe that we live in the last days where the church has no option but to unify, if we want to do excellent ministry for Jesus Christ. There are things that are happening in the world and coming upon this world in which we must unify as one in order to get the victory in Jesus. As I prepare to conclude, I want to leave you with the profound verses that David penned in Psalm 133.

Psalms 133:1-3 KJV

1 A Song of degrees of David. Behold, how good and how pleasant it is for brethren to dwell together in unity!

2 It is like the precious ointment upon the head, that ran down upon the beard, even Aaron's beard: that went down to the skirts of his garments;

3 As the dew of Hermon, and as the dew that descended upon the mountains of Zion: for there the LORD commanded the blessing, even life forevermore.

Here are a few points that are important for us to remember about unity.

1. Unity is good and pleasant.
2. Unity is compared to the precious anointing oil.
3. Unity is like dew that descends and refreshes all who embrace it.
4. Where there is unity and oneness, God commands the blessing, even life forevermore!

My prayer for everyone who reads this book is that the LORD Jesus Christ would give you wisdom and great understanding of the importance and power of unity. Let us not only be hearers of the Word, but doers of the Word, so that we can do great things in the Name of Jesus until he returns! May God Bless you

Notes

Strong, James. *The New Strong's Exhaustive Concordance of the Bible: With Main Concordance, Appendix to the Main Concordance, Hebrew and Aramaic Dictionary of the Old Testament, Greek Dictionary of the New Testament*. Nashville: T. Nelson, 1997.

Vallowe, Ed F. *Biblical Mathematics: Keys to Scripture Numerics: The Significance of Scripture Numbers Revealed in the Word of God*. Columbia, SC: Olive Press, 1998.

"Dictionary, Encyclopedia and Thesaurus." *The Free Dictionary*. Accessed October 22, 2018. http://www.thefreedictionary.com/.

"American Dictionary of the English Language." Webster's Dictionary 1828. Accessed November 05, 2018. http://webstersdictionary1828.com/.

"Overview - Adam Clarke Commentary." StudyLight.org. Accessed December 27, 2018. https://www.studylight.org/commentaries/acc.html.

Simons, Keith. Psalm 133 Commentary. Accessed December 27, 2018. http://www.usefulbible.com/songs-of-ascent/psalm-133.htm.

About the Author

Pastor Jamal E. Quinn is the Senior Pastor of Firm Foundation Christian Fellowship in Riverview, FL. He is a native of Louisville, Kentucky and a U.S. Navy veteran of 21 years.

He accepted the call into the ministry and was licensed as a Minister of the Gospel of Jesus Christ in 1999. In May 2002 - 2003, while serving in the military he was ordered to the Middle East with Special Operations Command Central Forward on a one-year assignment in Doha, Qatar. It was at this time in the desert, that the Lord called him to preach the Gospel and minister the Word of God in True Righteousness, Holiness, Deliverance and Truth.

In June 2003, he was assigned to Naval Air Station Jacksonville, Florida on another assignment. During this time he committed himself to a thorough and diligent study of the Holy Bible. In September of 2005, he retired after serving 21 years in the U.S. Navy.

In Oct 2005, he returned home to Riverview, Florida where the Lord led him to start a community Bible study by faith. Preaching and teaching the Gospel in his neighborhood to anyone that had an ear to hear. In Oct 2007, after faithfully conducting a Bible study group in his home, the Lord called Pastor Jamal and Prophetess Sheryl Quinn to plant Firm

Foundation Christian Fellowship in the community of Riverview.

Pastor Quinn is a visionary, shepherd, and watchman who preaches the Gospel of the Kingdom with passion, power and truth. Pastor Quinn's passion is teaching, exhorting and encouraging the Body of Christ to fulfill their God ordained destiny, and to live their lives as examples in Jesus Christ.

He received his Associate of Science Degree at Excelsior College, Albany, New York, and obtained his Bachelor of Arts in Pastoral Ministry from South Florida Bible College and Theological Seminary in Deerfield Beach, FL.

Pastor Quinn has been married to Co-Pastor and 1st Lady Sheryl Quinn, his high school sweetheart for over 33 years. For additional information on Pastor Quinn or other books, visit https://jamalquinn.com/ For additional information on Firm Foundation Christian Fellowship, visit https://www.firmfoundationcf.org

www.ingramcontent.com/pod-product-compliance
Lightning Source LLC
Chambersburg PA
CBHW071619040426
42452CB00009B/1397